GLEN ROCK PUBLIC LIBRARY
GLEN ROCK, N.J. 07452

Let's Get Lost in a Painting

by
ERNEST GOLDSTEIN

WINSLOW HOMER
The Gulf Stream

designed by Marsha Cohen

Garrard Publishing Company
Champaign, Illinois

Additional diagrams by Don Stacy

Robert Saunders, Series Consultant

Copyright © 1982 by Ernest Goldstein.

All rights reserved.

Library of Congress Cataloging in Publication Data

Goldstein, Ernest, 1933-
    Winslow Homer, The Gulf Stream.

    (Let's get lost in a painting ; v. 1)
    Summary: Analyzes one of the most famous sea paintings by the nineteenth century's outstanding artist of the American outdoors.
    1. Homer, Winslow, 1836-1910. Gulf Stream—Juvenile literature. [1. Homer, Winslow, 1836-1910. Gulf Stream. 2. Painting, American. 3. Art appreciation] I. Homer, Winslow, 1836-1910. II. Title. III. Series: Goldstein, Ernest, 1933-   . Let's get lost in a painting ; v. 1.
ND237.H7A65   1982   759.13   81-20055
ISBN 0-8116-1000-4   AACR2

Editorial and Production services by Cobb/Dunlop Inc.

Manufactured in the United States of America.

To the girls
Helen and Maura

and

To the boys
Adam and Joshua

Photo Acknowledgments

Winslow Homer *The Gulf Stream*
The Metropolitan Museum of Art, Wolfe Collection, 1906
Entire painting pages 2–3, 6, 11, 16, 24
Details pages 4–5, 7, 9, 12–13, 15, 19, 26, 34, 37, 39

Winslow Homer *Study for The Gulf Stream*
Courtesy of Cooper-Hewitt Museum, The Smithsonian Institution, National Museum of Design
page 19

The Ark and Homer's Studio (formerly the stable) at Prout's Neck, ca 1884
Homer Collection, Bowdoin College Museum of Art, Brunswick, Maine
page 21

Winslow Homer Working on *The Gulf Stream* in his Studio
Homer Collection, Bowdoin College Museum of Art, Brunswick, Maine
page 22

Katsushika Hokusai *The Great Wave of Kanagawa*
The Metropolitan Museum of Art, The Howard Mansfield Collection, Rogers Fund, 1936
page 26

Winslow Homer *Shark Fishing*
Private Collection, New York
page 27

Winslow Homer *The Gulf Stream*
Collection of The Art Institute of Chicago
page 28

Winslow Homer *Rum Cay*
Worcester Art Museum, Worcester, Massachusetts
page 28

John Singleton Copley *Watson and the Shark*
National Gallery of Art, Washington D.C., Ferdinand Lammot Belin Fund
page 30

Winslow Homer *A Visit from the Old Mistress*
National Museum of American Art (formerly National Collection of Fine Arts)
Smithsonian Institution
Entire painting page 33
Details page 34

Winslow Homer *West Point, Prout's Neck*
Sterling and Francine Clark Art Institute, Williamstown, Massachusetts
page 35

WINSLOW HOMER
The Gulf Stream

Did you ever look at a painting and say to yourself, "I like it. I don't know why, I just like it"? And did you ever wonder what the artist did to make you feel that way?

As you enter the world of Winslow Homer's The Gulf Stream, *you will seek answers to these questions and many others. The real fun will be in the challenge to look and find the answers yourself. They may be quite different from anyone else's. That is not important. In the end, only you will judge whether you like it—or even what it means. Before you begin, turn the page and study the painting.*

What's happening here? Storms, a shipwreck, and hungry sharks waiting for a human meal. But the sharks are not really waiting; one of them is trying to jump into the boat. That big one in front with the scary eye and jaws full of terrible teeth wants to leap right out of the picture and bite the viewer.

The ocean is full of sharks. How many do you see in the painting? Count them! One...two...three...maybe four or five? A hundred beneath the water possibly? Try again. That big one in front—is that his tail in the lower right corner? Or are there two different sharks? How can you tell? Place your finger on the head and trace the line into the water back to the tail. Still not sure? The artist wants you to think there are many sharks. Even when

the artist plays tricks with your eyesight, the answer is there. Some detective work is needed.

The clue is in the fins. Look at the illustration and find the different kinds of shark fins.

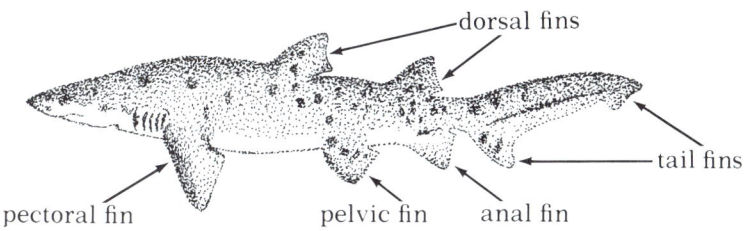

Now go back to that big shark in the front. The fins on top separated by the water are the dorsal fins. Below and near the mouth you can almost make out a pectoral fin. In the water is the pelvic fin, followed by an anal fin and the big lopsided tail swishing red spray.

There is one shark in front. A second shark is near the boat, again separated by the water. Can you name the big fin almost touching the cabin? You are right if you call it the pectoral. There is another pectoral fin—of a third

shark! You know what it is because the shape is the same as the large pectoral fin of the shark near the boat. Now, can you see the three sharks? Before reading on, try making your own sketch of them in the water. Which way are they moving? The illustration shown here is likely what the artist had in mind.

If your eye is really sharp, you can even tell the kind of shark. Find the tail of the shark near the boat. Trace the line of the fin and you will come to a funny hitch. That hitch is the mark of a sand shark—that and the round, pointed snout.

Now that you know the number of sharks you might ask "So what?" What does it tell you about the painting?

The answer is not in what you see, but how you look. You get the feeling of an ocean full of monsters. Yet, there are only three. Looking at a painting is like solving a puzzle. The artist has given the clues. Now you must find them.

If the sharks do not get the man, there is still more danger out there. Look at the ocean! The water is rough and the waves are high. In the right rear corner there is more trouble. Big trouble! A waterspout! A waterspout is a tornado on the water. Sailors have a very simple rule about them: DANGER, get away fast! That sailing ship on the left-hand side got the message. It is at full sail going as fast and as far away as possible.

Do you think the storm is coming toward the man in the boat, or has it already gone by? Waterspouts are tricky and follow no one direction. How can you tell, or *can* you tell? The boat tells a lot. A bowsprit is the large pole that holds the sail. Here, the bowsprit is broken. Sails are hanging over the boat and the rudder is gone. The boat is helpless, out of control and drifting. The man and his boat have been through a storm—perhaps caused by a watersprout.

Waterspouts are common in the Gulf Stream. Now, how do you know it is the Gulf Stream? Even if you do not know the title, the artist gives clues. First, the name of the boat painted on the back is *Anne of Key West.* Key West is at the tip of Florida. Second, sand sharks and flying fish—those specks of white to the right of the boat—are found in the Gulf Stream off the coast of Florida. Third, the Gulf Stream is marked by deep blue water that is much bluer than the ocean around it.

Winslow Homer finished painting *The Gulf Stream* in 1899. The date is in black at the lower left corner. From the very first time it was shown, people have been frightened by it. It is called a dramatic painting because you can "read" it like a drama or story—a horror story!

If the sharks or the storm do not get the man, there is still trouble. The boat could plow into a reef. That big white curlicue behind the boat may be caused by waves crashing over a coral reef. Or again, all alone, deserted by the only possible help—a ship going the other way—with no food or water, the man could starve to death. So, his end could be near. Anyway, that is what you see at

Florida

Key Largo

Key West

Florida Keys

Bahamas

first glance, and that is what everyone has always seen. The picture is frightening.

When the painting was first shown in a museum, a group of confused people wrote to Winslow Homer and asked him to explain what he meant. Homer gave the following answer: "The sharks and the boat are not important to the picture. They have been blown out to sea by a hurricane. The man on the boat, who seems so hot and dazed, will be rescued and live happily ever after."

What a strange thing to say! Naturally, nobody believed him then, and, to this day, people continue to think the worst. How is a happy ending possible when death seems so close? The man is at the mercy of Mother Nature, who does not seem to care. The ocean can be cruel—very cruel.

Why do people love a painting that gives them the chills? Homer says that the man will live happily ever after. Perhaps he was kidding—but maybe he wasn't. Remember, his letter said that the sharks and the boat were not important to the picture. So, what is the story about? When a great artist does a dramatic painting, he does not give you the whole story. He selects one moment, one special moment when time stands still on the canvas. It is the moment that puts you inside and tells everything—what happened and what will happen. Now, go back and find that moment.

If the ocean has danger, it also has great beauty. A woman once told another famous English ocean painter that she had never seen the colors of the water that he had put in his painting. The artist, J. M. Turner, said to her, "Ah, but don't you wish you could?" And that's the same feeling you get from the blues, blue greens, violets, sapphires and emeralds of *The Gulf Stream.*

Try to imagine where the sun is. You say it is not there? But it is. Sunlight is falling directly on the boat. Homer shows the position of the sun by means of shadow and color. If you wanted to discover that position through shadows, here is one possible solution. Study the diagram for help. You can see the shadow on the sugarcane,

the man, and the mast. The shadow on the sugarcane falls at an angle. If a line is drawn from the cane to the cabin cover, it moves up to the right. The shadows on the man point to the light overhead. When you line up these shadows with the mast, they all line up above his head. The sun is straight above.

Homer's use of brown is another clue to the position of the sun. There are dark browns, almost in shadow, on the side of the cabin and lower left side of the boat. There are sunny white browns on the upper part of the deck, and pink-and-white browns on top of the cabin and on the sailor's skin. If you go to the Metropolitan Museum of Art in New York and see the original painting, get close to it. You will see how much variety Homer put into his brown.

Homer knew the laws of color and understood that the best way to contrast the rich variety of browns was by the use of black and white. He often said that the proper use of black and white can suggest color. Now look at the shades of white. The tropical sun overhead is very strong. It is so hot that you can see white beads of perspiration on the man's dark skin. Direct sunlight is

falling on the warm whites of the sail, on the man's body, pants, and on the lower corner of the boat. The white becomes less bright when it is picked up on the flying fish and the sharks. Toward the waterspout the white looks cold, like the green of the crashing waves. Notice the solid white line between the blue-gray waterspout and the sailing ship. At first, the white border seems like the horizon, but it is not. It is probably foam coming off the waves whipped up by the winds of the storm. As your eyes pass the sailing ship to the left and return to the center of the picture, you can again pick up direct sunlight with flecks of warm white dancing on top of the waves.

The color in *The Gulf Stream* is one of the glories of American art—an achievement! A boat of brown is lightened by black and darkened by white against the rich blues of the sea. The blues are darkened at the crests of the waves and lightened by direct sunlight. The more you look, the more color you see. All that beauty should not have an unhappy ending.

That is what you see, but what does the painting say? What is all that red stuff in the water? Could it be blood? Is the man alone because another friend was thrown overboard? It looks like blood, but it is not. It is seaweed. Red seaweed comes into the Gulf Stream from the Gulf of Mexico. In this case it could have been dug up by the storm. On the other hand, there is that big red gash close to the mouth of the big shark. Mysterious—and frightening! Homer might have put it there to give a feeling of violence.

If all these terrible things might be happening to the man on the boat, how do you think he feels? What is going on inside his mind? Take another look, a very careful look! Read his face. Does he have the look of a man who has lost a battle? Does he seem frightened? Scared? Angry? Determined? Or just waiting for something to happen? Can you really tell?

A famous writer looked at the picture for a long time and came up with this idea: "The important point of this story is the man's distance from a shore or even a safe place. The man is still alive, but not for long. The picture is designed like a big trap ready to close. On one side of the trap are the sharks and on the other side, the waterspout. The man has not only lost the battle, but does

not even have any strength left to call for help from the other ship. Even if he escapes these dangers around him, he will probably starve from lack of food and water."

Do you agree? Is that what you see on the man's face? Take another look. What can you tell about him? He is very strong. From the way he is sitting, you can see the great strength in his arms and chest. The body is relaxed and he is resting on one elbow.

Notice how the artist has turned his head. From this position you can see determination in the powerful neck. And he is looking straight out to the side. That tells a lot. If he were a beaten man, a defeated man, he would be looking down. If he were looking up, he might be either desperate and praying to the heavens, or sure that help was coming. But the man is looking to the side! Whatever he is looking at, whatever he is thinking, remains a mystery. What you do know is that this is not the look of someone who has given up the battle.

Another reason Homer may have painted the man leaning and looking to the right is because he wanted you to look in that direction. If you do, you will see the flying fish which point to the waterspout. The waterspout leans toward the left—toward the sailing ship. The ship directs the eye back into the painting—back to the man. Which way do the sharks and the boat direct you to look? The big shark points left—but his fin points up right. The smaller shark points right. In a painting this is called "movement." The drawing shows the movement in the painting.

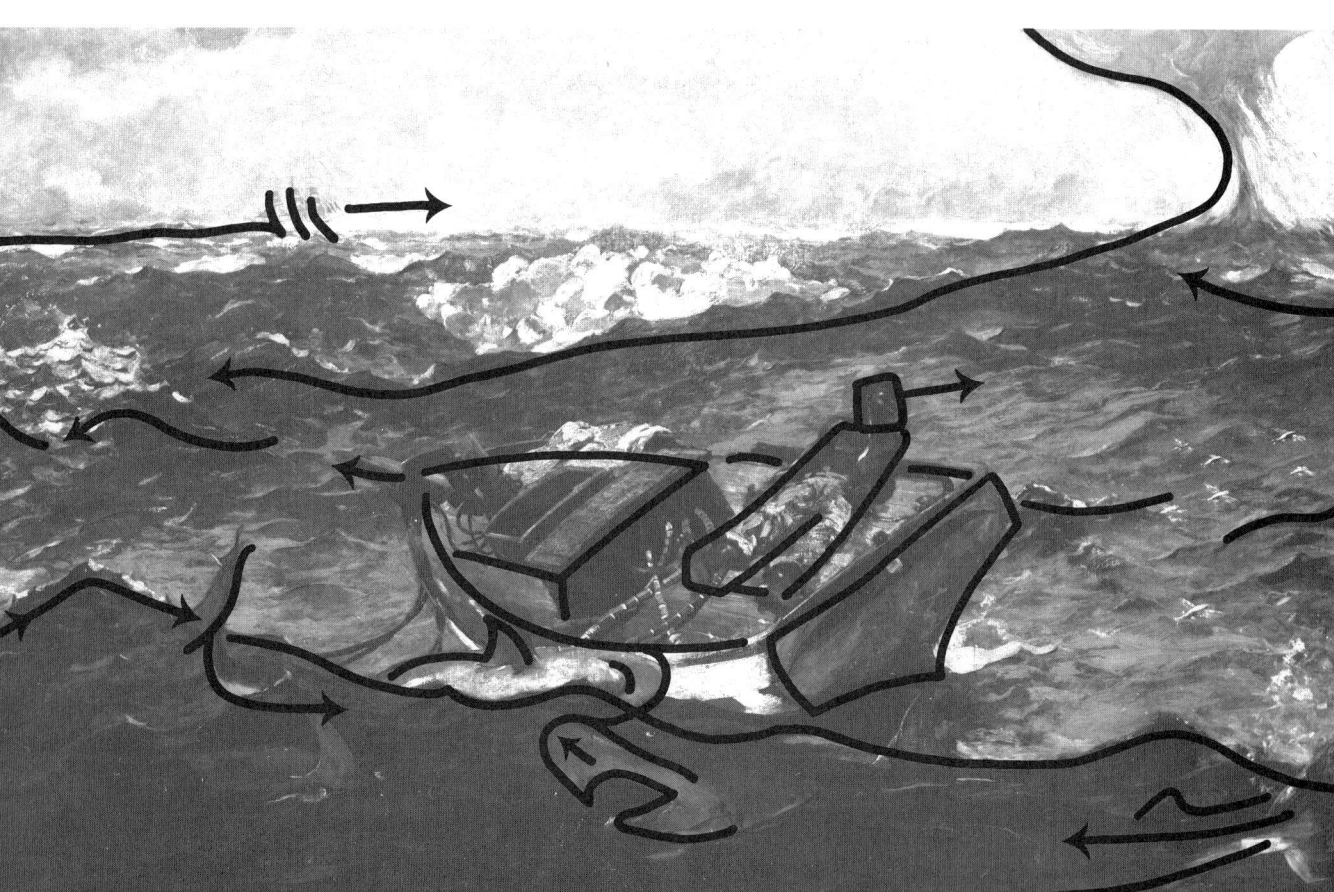

This man has been in trouble before, and perhaps in these very same waters. How can you know that? More detective work. How about the boat? What kind is it? A sailboat! But what kind of sailboat? You might say "What difference does it make? A boat is a boat." Not so. In this case, the sailboat is a very special kind, a smack boat sloop. Smack boats have a well or hole between the cabin and hatch to keep the fish. The illustration shows what the boat looked like before the storm, safe in the harbor. You can see all the fishing gear on the boat: fish pots, water barrels, nets, and conch shells.

Although these boats are no longer in use, they are part of the American heritage. Like the boat in the picture, they looked more like a tub. They were workboats, and the men who sailed them were always on the water.

There is a wonderful tradition about the brave sailors who worked on these boats around the Gulf Stream. These men were known for their strength and courage. They worked on the ocean day and night, year after year, and often went to sea in bad weather. The smack boat sailor was a great sailor. It was said that he could smell bad weather. He could read the clouds for signs of land beyond the horizon. He could even steer his boat by the formations of grass and coral in the seabed when out of sight of land.

The man in the painting was this kind of sailor. Now, one more look at his face and what do you see? Does *he* think he will make it? He has strength and courage. What else does the sailor have? Remember the sugarcane in his right hand? So he is not going to starve because sugarcane offers both food and water. His eyes could be on those flying fish and maybe, just maybe, he will catch a few. And, of course, it is possible that he may have some fish in the well.

Now can you figure out if the boat is sinking? Again, Homer gave the answer. Put your finger on the corner of the stern, or the back end. Trace the edge of the boat, including the space hidden by the shark. The line of the boat is above the water. It is not taking on water. In

sailor's language, the ship still has "integrity." This is the position Homer wanted. Compare it to an earlier study of the Gulf Stream. In this work the boat is taking on water. In the final picture it is not clear. Although it is helpless and tipping it is not sinking, yet. (page 19)

In fact there are several problems in this picture that are not clear. For example, sharks never come to the top of the water during a storm. They stay far below. The water is rough, but it still might not be made so by the waterspout. Now things really get tough. Homer knew sharks and he knew that the sand shark does not attack human beings. In a frenzy, however, sharks attack anything, and there is that big gash on the shark's mouth. So you still really do not know what is going on.

Homer's letter said there was something else. Another story. In fact there are two dramas. The first one is outside the man—on the ocean. The second one, inside the man, begins with his relaxed position and the bold look on his face. What you think might happen changes the moment you are inside the painting. Now the question becomes: what does *he* think will happen. What is on the sailor's mind? Or another way—what was on Homer's mind? For that answer you must go to the history of this artist and how he did his work.

Winslow Homer was born in Boston in 1826 and died in Prouts Neck, Maine, in 1910. During his lifetime he had become the outstanding artist of the American outdoors. His paintings of hunting scenes in the Adirondacks, fishermen on dories, and waves smashing against the rocky coast of Maine are now part of the American heritage. When the Metropolitan Museum of Art in New York bought *The Gulf Stream,* it paid him the highest amount he ever received for a painting, $4,500.00—a great sum of money in those days.

Homer was a man who liked to be alone. And so, to this day, very little is known about him. He lived like a pioneer. At the age of forty, he left city life and moved to a lonely ocean village, Prouts Neck, Maine. He kept away from people, even art critics and buyers, and talked to no one about himself or his work.

When he became quite old, the writer William Howe Downes asked him for information for a biography. Homer answered: "I think that it would probably kill me to have such a thing appear, and as the most interesting part of my life is of no concern to the public, I must decline."

This was not Homer's first refusal. In the letter about the meaning of *The Gulf Stream,* he had written the following thought: "You ask me for a full description of my picture *The Gulf Stream.* I regret very much that I have painted a picture that *requires* any description." But the meaning is not clear and the picture does require "description." There are two valuable clues outside this work. For help you can go to his other paintings and to some important events during his lifetime.

You can start your detective work with a photograph. There is only one photograph of Homer in his studio. He is standing in front of *The Gulf Stream.* How big do you think the painting is? Here is a clue: Homer was approximately five-feet, six-inches tall. The painting is twenty-eight by forty-nine inches. If you measure a rectangle on

the floor, you can get the size of the real painting. That photograph tells you much. You can see that the painting is unfinished. In the background it is possible to make out two waterspouts. There is still no white spray over the tail, and the waves are not fully painted.

How long does it take to finish a painting? When did Homer know that the work was done—that the color, design, and idea all fit together? He started *The Gulf Stream* in 1897, and finished it in 1899—two years later. During these two years the painting was shown and returned to him for more change. Why? Even after he worked out the details, Homer considered the painting a failure if the viewer did not understand the idea. His work was not simply a photograph of what he saw, but rather his way of expressing feelings and ideas. At that time people did not understand what he was trying to do.

Today viewers consider the painting "great." You can look at it time and again and always find something new—a little detail, not seen before, to add to your pleasure. For example, sharks really do not have teeth like the ones in the painting. But who cares? When the shark opens its mouth, you see jaws but Homer painted *maws*. MAWS, now that is a word! *Maws* means "appetite" in a very special sense—the appetite of a wild, man-eating creature. And that is what you see and feel—the appetite of a shark too close to the man in the boat, ready to swallow the victim whole.

The ability to describe a thing and give it such powerful feelings is the inspiration of the artist. This was Homer's gift: to describe and to communicate with feeling. If you use your imagination, you can see how he gives feeling to the shape of the ocean. Once he puts terror into his picture, the whole design cries out "Dan-

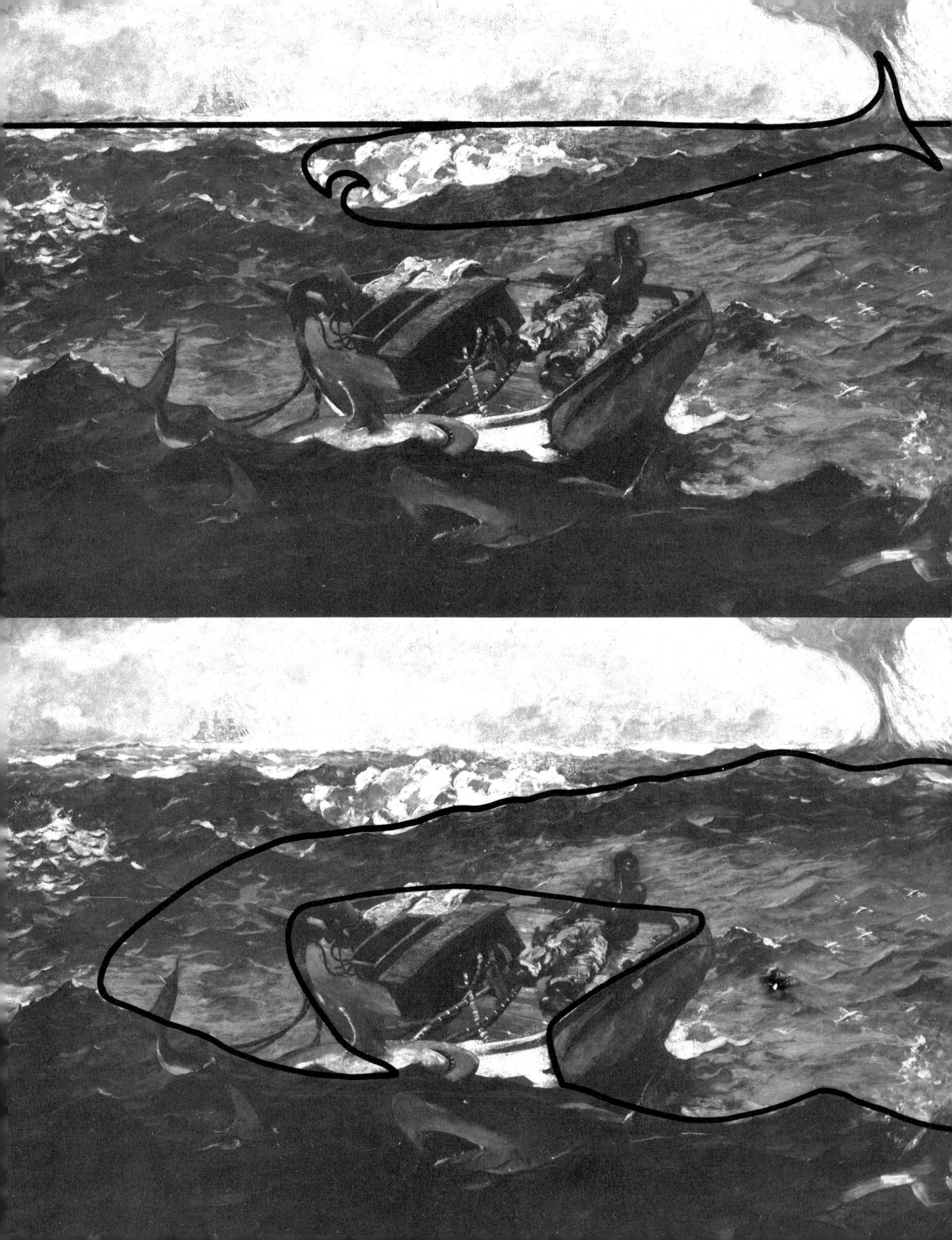

ger!" The illustrations show how the frightening image of the shark repeats itself in the design. In the first illustration, the water forms a pattern of the huge fish with its tail as the waterspout. In the second illustration, the lines of the big waves meet to form one large, terrifying shark with the boat in its maws. The design becomes one shape—one emotion—one overpowering feeling—TERROR!

It is likely that Homer had seen that technique used before. In 1854, Admiral Perry made his famous trip to Japan and opened its ports to the world. Soon after, sailors brought back art prints of the Japanese masters. America and Europe suddenly discovered Japanese art. Hokusai was one of the greatest of the Japanese artists. Homer knew his picture *The Great Wave of Kanagawa.* In the illustration you can see the same lacy lines of the waves. Hokusai's large wave rolls over into curlicues—much like Homer's design of the reef. The technique is Japanese, a pretty ornament on top of the water. Hokusai's wave looks like a monster reaching out over the men in the boats, like Homer's wave, ready to swallow up the sailor. But it is remarkable that in the center of both works there is such a quiet feeling. In Hokusai's a peaceful Mount Fuji; in Homer's the relaxed body of the man. (page 26)

The Gulf Stream was not the first time Homer had painted sharks. He first went to the Bahamas in 1885 and soon after did a watercolor called *Shark Fishing.* Notice the power of the man using only a small line to battle the monster. Homer's watercolors and paintings of the tropics are remarkable for their strong colors and dramatic stories of man's war with nature. His pictures have no

pity for man or beast. Now look at two more works: *Rum Cay* and an early study of *The Gulf Stream.* (page 28)

The watercolor *Rum Cay* tells a brutal story. Look at the strength of the man: the powerful head, the huge chest, the whole body excitedly bent toward one object—the turtle. The turtle is going to lose. In 1899, Homer painted a watercolor which he also named *The Gulf Stream.* Notice that the lower side of the boat is almost in water, while the man is high above the cabin with his shirt on. These earlier works can be considered the be-

ginning of a drama not finished until 1899 in *The Gulf Stream.*

The first shark Winslow Homer saw could have been in *Brook Watson and the Shark* (1778) by John Singleton Copley. Homer grew up around Boston. When he was very young, his parents knew how well he could draw. They also knew it was very important for him to see the work of other artists. Since *Brook Watson and the Shark* hung in the Boston Athenaeum, it is possible that young Winslow saw it many times. *The Gulf Stream* and Copley's painting are somewhat alike. Copley placed the shark right in front, leaping out of the water. Homer's shark has the same huge mouth and knife-sharp teeth as Copley's. In both pictures the shark has a frightening eye that seems almost human. But you can find something even more interesting in comparing the two: look at the faces of the men in Copley's painting. They are all frightened and upset, except one man in the center. There stands a black sailor, calm, confident, and strong before the danger. (page 30)

There is something else about the Copley work that Homer knew. Brook Watson, the man in the water, had been attacked by a shark. But there was a happy ending after his terrible adventure. Later, Watson became Lord Mayor of London and paid Copley to paint his attack by the shark. Maybe this is what Homer meant when he said *The Gulf Stream* had a happy ending.

Homer had an uneasy feeling about *The Gulf Stream.* Before he finished, he wrote to his agent that he did not want "the public to poke its nose into the picture." Homer knew his people. That same public was not used to seeing such terror in paintings. He was sure people would get the wrong idea, and they did. Over the years

he painted fishermen catching sharks. When the audience first saw *The Gulf Stream,* many people said, "Now it's the shark's turn to catch the fisherman."

At the very first showing of *The Gulf Stream,* art critics were divided in their reports. One writer was shocked by such an awful subject. Another could not understand why "the ship was not wet with seawater" or "how the man kept himself from sliding down the boat." This last critic looked at the painting as if it were a photograph. He missed the idea in every way. With time, these kinds of questions have been answered. But there are other questions about the painting that still deserve attention. Here is one: Does it make any difference to the picture or to the story if the man is white or black? There is no one answer.

This question was often asked in a different way: Why did Homer put a black man on the boat? What a sad question, sad because of the date—1899! The Civil War had ended in 1865. Thirty-four years had passed. It is sad because the fight for equal rights in art had not ended. Most paintings treated blacks as objects only, not as people. The Copley painting was the great exception. Before the Civil War, most paintings of blacks showed them either suffering in slavery, happily dancing, or playing banjos. Now, Homer puts his man in a boat in the middle of the ocean at the center of his picture. And what a magnificent human being he is! This man is not a slave. What appears at first glance to be a ball and chain on his left is an illusion. The left hand is hooked onto the belt loop of his pants.

Do you think it makes any difference to the story if the man is black or white? Maybe, but no one is sure. Did it make any difference to Homer? The artist cannot lie! A great work of art is one man's way of telling the truth. There is always a reason for his choice of color, although you may never fully understand it. There are two events, however, in Homer's lifetime that tell a lot about his sense of color. They are the Civil War and the publication of a remarkable book, *The Laws of Contrast of Colour* by M. E. Chevreul.

During the Civil War, Homer was a war artist for *Harper's* magazine. He made several trips to the war front and sometimes he saw the fighting. At the front, he made sketches and then came back to New York to finish the drawings. He was what is now called an artist-reporter.

In 1875, ten years after the Civil War had ended, Homer made a trip to Petersburg, Virginia. That year is important not only in the life of the artist, but also in the history of American painting. Homer had been to Petersburg before, in 1865, after a terrible battle. He went back in 1875 and decided to live in the black neighborhood and paint. The war had been over for a long time, but there was still hate. Some white troublemakers from Petersburg were angry. Homer paid no attention. One day, a group of toughies decided to get him and drive him out of town. One rough-looking fellow came up and threatened him. Homer said, "I looked him in the eyes, as mother told us to look at a wild cow," and the toughie ran away. Homer did not know what happened. But a Texan, who had hidden under the porch, explained that he ran because he thought Homer had a gun in each hand and was ready to shoot him. After that, no one bothered him again. He painted a whole series of works showing blacks as black Americans—at work, in church, at play —no different from white Americans except for the color of their skin.

During his time in Petersburg, Homer painted *The Visit of the Old Mistress.* The mistress has come back to visit with the ex-slaves. What did she expect to find? What does her face tell you? She seems confused because she is not getting the friendship that she might have wanted. What do you see in the faces of the black

women? Look closely at the eyes and mouths of the ex-slaves. You can see dignity, but also scorn. What do you see on the face of the large black woman in the middle? Does her look remind you of one you have seen somewhere else? Before you answer, go back to the face of the man in *The Gulf Stream.* Compare the two faces and decide for yourself.

On the lower left corner of *The Gulf Stream* are the date and the signature of the artist in black. From our earlier study, you know how Homer used black and white to contrast color. To paint rich colors of *The Gulf Stream,* a man could spend a lifetime: first in seeing such beauty and then putting it on canvas for others to enjoy. Sometimes the work was slow and tiring. After *West Point, Prouts Neck,* Homer described his technique. "The picture is painted *fifteen minutes after sunset*—not one minute before—since up to that minute the clouds would have their edges lighted with a brilliant glow of color—but now, in this picture, the sun has gone beyond their range and they are in shadow. The light is from the sky in this picture. You can see that it took many days of careful study to get this effect with the sea and tide just right."

Anytime you see his work you can study color and shadow and always figure out the time of day. He once said about a picture he was painting, "I work hard every afternoon from 4:30 to 4:40 (ten minutes), that being the limit of the light in the picture."

Besides those ten minutes, Homer spent hours and years studying the effects of sunlight on color. You might ask how he knew that the colors he saw were true. A little more detective work!

Homer kept a book which he read and reread. He once even called it "my bible." The name of that book is *The Laws of Contrast of Colour* written by M. E. Chevreul. Chevreul, a French scientist, published his work in

1839. It was translated into English in 1858. Ever since the book appeared, it has influenced everything from housing to flower arrangement and furniture. By reading Chevreul's experiments, artists had a guide to study the sun's effects on light and color.

Homer had mastered Chevreul's laws. He knew that every object brightens if placed against a shadow. He understood how black makes brown look light, or blue look dark.

Now, go back again and see how Homer used Chevreul's law of color contrast. Brown is a dark color; blue, a light one. Find the black in the painting. You see it in the empty space in the cabin and in the hatch, on the man's head, on the bottom of his pants, and around the dark border of the boat. Within the boat, the dark browns get lighter, while outside the boat the light blues get darker. In art that is called depth of color. The effects are surprising because the more you look, the more shades of colors you will find.

An artist once asked Homer if he changed the colors he saw. Homer, shocked by the question, answered, "Never, Never. When I have selected a thing, I paint it exactly as it appears." Then he added something interesting: "Of course, you must not paint everything you see. You must wait, and wait patiently, for the wonderful to come and hope to have the sense to see it."

Waiting patiently is one way of describing Homer's life and work. His house at Prouts Neck was right on the ocean. From his window, he could study the waves rolling in against the coast, sending off sprays of light and color. He even built a "paint house" that he could move close to the ocean in a storm. His only interest was his work.

Another artist tells a story of his visit to Homer. A storm had come up and Homer said they had to see it— at once! "During my visit, a storm swept the coast. No one

at Prouts Neck, not even the oldest people, could remember such bad weather. The wind blew a gale. The rain was heavy. There were clouds of mist over the rocks and the sound of the ocean rose over the waves." Homer was excited. They put on raincoats and walked along the shore. They had to hold on to the rocks, or the wind would have knocked them down. Homer watched the clouds for a change in the weather. It was for this moment that he had waited. For this he was always ready, with his paintbrush in his hand. For these moments Homer lived and remained alone.

There is no one answer to the question of why the man in the boat is black. Homer saw a lone black sailor in a Bahamian sloop and painted him. But a Winslow Homer work includes his genius, his life, and his vision. Homer's vision opens the eye to the visual splendor in nature, and it challenges the mind to understand this man. This black American is an example of people who have faced danger before and have survived.

You still don't know what will happen to the sailor. Take one more look and figure out which way the boat is drifting. Beneath the broken mast a rope hangs in the water. It seems to be fastened to something below the wave, perhaps a sea anchor. Although hidden from view, something there is almost pulling the boat, or even guiding it. The boat is moving between the waves and the storm into the beautiful, blue water. Perhaps into safety? Something unknown is directing it. But what?

You do not know because Homer did not want you to. Perhaps he himself did not know.

You went against the artist's wish and poked your nose into his painting. You went looking for the moment that would give you the key to the puzzle. And what did you find? Another puzzle! Although you still do not know

the ending you do know that it will be different from what you had expected.

When you are led to expect one thing and something else happens, that is called "irony." It would be visual irony if the beautiful ocean were to destroy the brave sailor. It would be dramatic irony if he were close to land and could not reach it.

But there are other ironies in this masterpiece. There is the irony of the Gulf Stream itself. In Homer's time, very little was known about "the river of blue." Ponce de Leon, the explorer, first described it; sailors navigated it; and scientists—even Benjamin Franklin, made charts of the currents. But in spite of all the effort and study, the Gulf Stream remained a mystery. Very little was known about where it began and ended, or what part it played in the ocean's flow. It is an irony that people try so hard to understand and still know so little about the Gulf Stream, the end of the story, or life itself for that matter. Like the mystery in the boat we, too, do not know the future.

It is now many years later. *The Gulf Stream* hangs in the Metropolitan Museum, and still haunts the viewer. So why do people love this painting even as it chills them and makes the future as scary as the eye of the shark?

The answer to this question is the key to the mystery. The horror is there. And yet one man's calm and courage give to the work a strength and dignity—and perhaps even faith. He is alone against the elements, but not defeated.

Like the man in the boat, Homer was alone. We are all alone, black and white, when the real trouble comes; when the monsters come out of the deep into our dreams. Alone when the world closes in on us; alone—adrift in currents of doubts—fearful about tomorrow. But that sailor knows something. Whatever it is, he is strong enough to look away from terror. In his look is the final irony. Homer was able to scare everyone who looked at *The Gulf Stream.* Everyone except the one man who could not be frightened—the man in the boat.

And who is that man in the boat? He is every one of us.

NOV 1992